Power Partnerships: Mastering the Art of Business Growth Through Partnership Recruiting

B. Vincent

Published by RWG Publishing, 2023.

While every precaution has been taken in the preparation of this book, the publisher assumes no responsibility for errors or omissions, or for damages resulting from the use of the information contained herein.

POWER PARTNERSHIPS: MASTERING THE ART OF BUSINESS GROWTH THROUGH PARTNERSHIP RECRUITING

First edition. April 11, 2023.

Copyright © 2023 B. Vincent.

Written by B. Vincent.

Also by B. Vincent

Affiliate Marketing
Affiliate Marketing
Affiliate Marketing

Standalone
Business Employee Discipline
Affiliate Recruiting
Business Layoffs & Firings
Business and Entrepreneur Guide
Business Remote Workforce
Career Transition
Project Management
Precision Targeting
Professional Development
Strategic Planning
Content Marketing
Imminent List Building
Getting Past GateKeepers
Banner Ads
Bookkeeping
Bridge Pages
Business Acquisition

Business Bogging
Business Communication Course
Marketing Automation
Better Meetings
Business Conflict Resolution
Business Culture Course
Conversion Optimization
Creative Solutions
Employee Recruitment
Startup Capital
Employee Incentives
Employee Mentoring
Followership
Servant Leadership
Human Resources
Team Building
Freelancing
Funnel Building
Geo Targeting
Goal Setting
Immanent List Building
Lead Generation
Leadership Course
Leadership Transition
Leadership vs Management
LinkedIn Ads
LinkedIn Marketing
Messenger Marketing
New Management
Newsfeed Ads
Search Ads
Online Learning
Sales Webinars

Side Hustles
Split Testing
Twitter Timeline Advertising
Earning Additional Income Through Side Hustles: Begin Earning Money Immediately
Making a Living Through Blogging: Earn Money Working From Home
Create Bonuses for Affiliate Marketing: Your Success Is Encompassed by Your Bonuses
Internet Marketing Success: The Most Effective Traffic-Driving Strategies
JV Recruiting: Joint Ventures Partnerships and Affiliates
Secrets to List Building
Step-by-Step Facebook Marketing: Discover How To Create A Strategy That Will Help You Grow Your Business
Banner Advertising: Traffic Can Be Boosted by Banner Ads
Affiliate Marketing
Improve Your Marketing Strategy with Internet Marketing
Outsourcing Helps You Save Time and Money
Choosing the Right Content and Marketing for Social Media
Make Products That Will Sell
Launching a Product for Affiliate Marketing
Pinterest as a Marketing Tool
Power Partnerships: Mastering the Art of Business Growth Through Partnership Recruiting

Table of Contents

Chapter 1: The Power of Partnerships: A Game-Changing Growth Strategy 1

Chapter 2: The Art of Partnership Recruiting: Finding Your Ideal Business Allies 5

Chapter 3: Defining Your Partnership Goals: What Do You Want to Achieve? 9

Chapter 4: Building a Partnership Network: Expanding Your Reach and Influence 13

Chapter 5: Crafting Your Partnership Pitch: Making a Strong First Impression 17

Chapter 6: Nurturing Your Partnerships: Cultivating Strong Relationships 21

Chapter 7: Overcoming Partnership Challenges: Resolving Conflict and Disagreements 25

Chapter 8: Measuring Partnership Success: How to Determine if It's Working 29

Chapter 9: Growing Your Business with Strategic Partnerships: Success Stories and Lessons Learned 33

Chapter 10: The Dos and Don'ts of Partnership Recruiting: Best Practices for Building Strong Alliances 37

Chapter 11: Creating Win-Win Partnerships: How to Ensure Mutually Beneficial Agreements 41

Chapter 12: The Role of Trust in Successful Partnerships: Building Rapport and Respect 43

Chapter 13: Finding the Right Partners: Identifying the Right Fit for Your Business 47

Chapter 14: Collaborating for Growth: Partnering with Competitors and Complementary Businesses 51

Chapter 15: The Legal Side of Partnerships: Understanding Contracts and Agreements.. 55

Chapter 16: Leveraging Partnerships for Marketing Success: Collaborative Campaigns and Strategies 57

Chapter 17: The Importance of Communication in Partnerships: Ensuring Clear and Consistent Dialogue 61

Chapter 18: The Future of Partnership Recruiting: Trends and Predictions for the Evolving Business Landscape... 65

Chapter 19: Scaling Your Business with Partnerships: How to Build a Network for Sustainable Growth 69

Chapter 20: Creating a Partnership Culture: Encouraging Collaboration and Innovation in Your Business 73

Chapter 1: The Power of Partnerships: A Game-Changing Growth Strategy

Businesses can grow and broaden their reach more effectively through the formation of strategic partnerships. They are able to assist businesses in achieving their common objectives by utilizing the capabilities, resources, and networks of one another. The power of partnerships as a game-changing growth strategy will be the topic of discussion in this chapter, as will the ways in which businesses can benefit from collaborating with other businesses.

Joint ventures, strategic alliances, and co-marketing agreements are just a few examples of the myriad of ways in which partnerships can be structured. All of these business collaborations have one thing in common: they involve two or more companies working together toward a common goal. When executed effectively, partnerships have the potential to yield a number of benefits, including entry into new markets, elevated levels of brand recognition, and cost savings.

Access to untapped markets is among the most significant benefits that can accrue from forming strategic alliances. When two companies decide to form a partnership, they bring together their respective customer bases, which results in the creation of a larger pool of potential customers. For instance, a company that specializes in technology may form a strategic alliance with a store that specializes in retail sales in order to sell their products in-store. Both companies benefit from the partnership: the retail company is given access to cutting-edge technology, and the technology firm is given access to an expanded customer base. This symbiotic relationship has the potential to bring in additional revenue for both of the involved companies.

The visibility of a brand can also be increased through partnerships. Businesses have the opportunity to expose their brand to new audiences through collaboration with other companies, which can contribute to the development of their reputation and the expansion of their market share. As an illustration, a cosmetics company might collaborate with a lifestyle blogger in order to produce a series of sponsored articles. It is possible that the audience of the blogger has never heard of the beauty brand before; however, thanks to the partnership, they will be able to learn about the brand and the products that it offers.

Another advantage of forming partnerships is the reduction in costs. When two businesses collaborate on a project or an initiative, they have the opportunity to split the costs that are associated with it. This can encompass anything and everything, from research and development to marketing and advertising. For the purpose of creating a new item, for instance, a company that manufactures goods might collaborate with a company that specializes in technology. Both businesses are able to bring the product to market more quickly and at a lower cost if they share the costs of the product's research and development.

In addition to these advantages, partnerships can also assist businesses in maintaining their competitive edge in an increasingly cutthroat market. Businesses can give themselves an advantage over their rivals by forming strategic alliances with other organizations and drawing on the capabilities and resources of their business partners. For instance, a small business may choose to form a partnership with a larger company in order to gain access to the resources that the larger company possesses, such as their technology and their expertise.

Nevertheless, there are difficulties involved in forming partnerships. In order to ensure the success of the partnership, it is essential to select the appropriate partner, to have clear objectives, and to establish clear communication. In the following chapters, we will delve into each of these aspects in greater detail and provide advice that can be put into practice by companies that are looking to create successful partnerships.

In a nutshell, partnerships are a game-changing growth strategy that can provide businesses with access to new markets, increased brand awareness, decreased costs, and a competitive advantage. Partnerships can also provide businesses with the opportunity to save money. Businesses are able to more effectively accomplish their goals and make use of the resources available to them when they work together with other businesses. To guarantee the success of the partnership, it is necessary to select the appropriate partner, to define the goals of the partnership, and to establish open lines of communication.

Chapter 2: The Art of Partnership Recruiting: Finding Your Ideal Business Allies

---

Finding the right person to work with is absolutely necessary for a prosperous partnership. Finding other businesses that have the same goals, ideals, and clientele is an essential part of developing successful partnership recruitment strategies. In this chapter, we will go over how to find the ideal business allies for you and provide some practical advice for efficiently recruiting new partnership candidates.

Establishing your objectives serves as the initial step in the recruitment process for partnerships. What are some of the goals that you have for a potential partnership? Are you interested in penetrating new markets, elevating the profile of your brand, or lowering your operating expenses? If you are aware of your objectives, you will be better able to locate companies that can assist you in achieving those objectives.

Next, consider your values. What is essential to your company, and what core beliefs do you hold in common with potential business partners? For instance, if your company is dedicated to the concept of sustainability, you may wish to collaborate with other businesses that have the same level of environmental consciousness as you do.

The intended audience is yet another essential factor to take into account. Who is the perfect client for your business, and who does the potential business partner cater to? It is absolutely necessary to have overlapping target audiences in order for a partnership to be successful. This ensures that both companies will reap the benefits of the partnership by increasing their exposure to new customers.

After you have a crystal clear understanding of your objectives, your core values, and your ideal customers, you can start looking for potential business partners. Participating in events for networking and conferences held within one's industry is one way to accomplish this goal. These events offer the chance to converse with other proprietors of businesses and acquire information regarding their operations.

You can also locate possible business partners through the use of social media. Engage with the content produced by businesses that you feel align with both your values and your target audience and follow them. Building relationships with prospective partners and identifying opportunities for joint ventures can both benefit from this.

Referral networks are yet another method that can be utilized to locate potential business partners. Make sure you solicit recommendations from your current partners, customers, and colleagues in the industry. They might have connections to other companies that would make a good addition to your partnership.

It is essential to conduct research before evaluating potential partners in a business venture. If you want to learn more about their company, check out their website, social media presence, and reviews left by previous customers. This will help you determine whether their goals and values are congruent with your own, as well as whether their target audience is similar to your own.

Assessing the previous work of a potential business partner is another essential step. Have they previously collaborated with other companies and achieved their goals? Have there been any failed partnerships on their part? By learning about their previous collaborations, you can better evaluate whether or not they would be a good fit for your company.

It is absolutely necessary to have a well-defined pitch before approaching potential business partners. Included in this should be an explanation of why you believe forming a partnership would be beneficial, as well as what you can bring to the partnership and what you hope to achieve.

In a nutshell, the art of partnership recruiting can be summed up as the process of locating businesses that share your goals, target audience, and core values. When determining whether or not a potential partner is a good fit for your business, it is critical to have a firm grasp on your goals and to conduct thorough due diligence. In order to find potential partners, you should participate in networking events, use social media, and leverage referral networks. When approaching prospective business partners, be sure to have a well-thought-out pitch prepared that details both what you can contribute to the partnership and what you want to accomplish through it.

Chapter 3: Defining Your Partnership Goals: What Do You Want to Achieve?

It is essential to define your partnership's goals in order to have any chance of having a prosperous one. What are some goals that you have for the partnership that you hope to accomplish? In this chapter, we will discuss how to define your partnership's goals and provide practical advice for creating a plan that aligns with those goals. In addition, we will look at some examples of successful partnerships.

The first thing you need to do in order to define the objectives of your partnership is to decide what it is that you want to accomplish. This could involve entering a new market, raising consumers' awareness of the brand, or lowering operating expenses. It is essential to have a comprehensive understanding of your goals in order to locate the ideal business partner and devise a strategy that is congruent with those objectives.

After you have decided what you want to accomplish, the next step is to figure out how you will evaluate your level of success. How will you measure progress, and what metrics will you use? This may include the amount of sales, traffic to the website, or customer engagement. If you have a crystal clear understanding of how you will measure success, it will be much easier for you to evaluate the efficiency of the partnership and stay on track with your goals.

It is also essential to give some thought to the timetable for accomplishing your objectives. How long do you anticipate the partnership will continue for, and what key achievements do you hope to accomplish during its course? If you have a detailed timeline, it will be easier for you to keep your attention on the task at hand and ensure that you are making headway toward achieving your goals.

It is essential to include all relevant stakeholders in the process of defining the goals you want to achieve through your partnership. This applies to both your team and the team of your partner, in addition to any other parties involved in the partnership. Everyone involved in the partnership ought to have a crystal clear understanding of the partnership's goals as well as the expectations placed on them.

The establishment of a partnership agreement is one strategy for ensuring that all parties are on the same page. In this, the partnership's goals, a timeline for achieving those goals, and the criteria by which success will be measured should be outlined. Additionally, it should detail the responsibilities of each party, as well as any financial or legal arrangements that have been made.

When defining the goals of your partnership, potential risks and difficulties are another important factor to take into consideration. What are the potential challenges that might prevent you from accomplishing your goals, and how do you plan to overcome these challenges if they arise? It is essential to have a strategy prepared in advance for resolving any issues that may crop up during the course of the partnership.

Being adaptable is another quality that should be prioritized when defining the objectives of your partnership. As the partnership develops, you might discover that the goals you set or the timeline you established need to be modified. It is essential to maintain a flexible mindset in order to keep moving forward and make progress toward the objectives you have set for yourself.

In conclusion, determining the objectives of your partnership is an essential step in the process of forming a fruitful collaboration. It is essential to have a crystal clear understanding of what it is you want to accomplish, how you will determine whether or not you were successful, and the timeline for accomplishing your goals. Involve all of the relevant stakeholders in the process, draft up a partnership agreement, and be ready to address any potential risks or difficulties that may arise. Maintain a flexible attitude and be open to revising your plan in order to increase the likelihood that you will meet your objectives.

Chapter 4: Building a Partnership Network: Expanding Your Reach and Influence

It is essential to build a network of partnership relationships in order to extend your reach and influence. A partnership network is a group of companies with which you work together toward the accomplishment of common objectives. In this chapter, we will discuss how to build a partnership network and provide practical advice for creating a network that can assist you in achieving your goals. This chapter will also cover how to build a partnership network that can help you achieve your goals.

The first thing you need to do in order to begin constructing a partnership network is to locate businesses that have similar values, goals, and audiences in mind. To accomplish this, you will need to conduct research and network with other professionals in order to find companies that are a good fit for your partnership network.

Attending industry conferences and other events geared toward networking is one way to locate potential business allies. These events offer the chance to converse with other proprietors of businesses and acquire information regarding their operations. You can also use social media to identify potential partners. Engage with the content of businesses that you find to share your values and audience, and follow those businesses.

Referral networks are yet another method that can be utilized to locate potential business partners. Make sure you solicit recommendations from your current partners, customers, and colleagues in the industry. They might have connections to other companies that would make a good addition to your partnership network.

It is essential to take into consideration the values, goals, and target audience of potential partners for your network when conducting your evaluation. Are they compatible with your company, and can you work with them to achieve goals that you both have in common? Assessing the previous work of a potential business partner is another essential step. Have they previously formed successful partnerships with other companies, and will their participation in your network be beneficial to its overall success?

After you have determined the potential partners for your network, the next step is to establish communication that is unmistakable. This includes defining the goals and expectations of your partnership, as well as determining how you will measure the partnership's success. In addition to this, it is essential to lay out a timetable for accomplishing your goals and to define key milestones along the way.

When establishing a network of partnerships, it is essential to be receptive to the possibility of collaboration and to seek out ways in which both parties can benefit from the relationship. This means combining forces in terms of resources, expertise, and networks in order to accomplish common goals. Because the requirements of your network may shift over time, it is essential to maintain a degree of versatility and adaptability.

It is essential to have a well-defined strategy for the management of your partnership network in order to guarantee the success of the network. This includes things like determining who will be responsible for what, setting up channels of communication, and developing a structure for making decisions. In addition to this, it is essential to conduct regular audits of the performance of your network and to make adjustments as required.

In conclusion, it is essential to acknowledge the value of your partnership network and to spread the word about it to other people. This involves letting your customers and other people in your network know about the successes you've had and promoting the businesses that are part of your network. This can assist in the development of your reputation and the expansion of your influence within your sector of the market.

In conclusion, developing a network of partnerships is necessary if you want to extend your sphere of influence and reach. It is important to identify businesses that share your values, goals, and target audience in order to build a partnership network that is successful. Additionally, it is important to establish clear communication, be open to collaboration, and have a clear plan for managing the network. If you want to have more influence within your field, you should evaluate the usefulness of your network on a regular basis and then promote it to other people.

Chapter 5: Crafting Your Partnership Pitch: Making a Strong First Impression

It is critical to develop a compelling partnership pitch in order to leave a positive first impression with potential business partners. Your presentation ought to communicate, in a way that is both clear and succinct, the benefits of the partnership as well as what it is that you bring to the table. In this chapter, we will go over the best practices for formulating a partnership proposal that leaves an enduring and favorable first impression.

The first thing you should do when developing your business proposal for a partnership is to determine your goals. What are some goals that you have for the partnership that you hope to accomplish? This should serve as the primary focal point of your presentation because it conveys the value that the partnership can bring to the other company in question.

After you have figured out what you want to accomplish, the next step is to consider what you have to offer the other company. This may include providing the other company with access to your customer base, your expertise in a specific field, or resources that can assist the other company in accomplishing their goals. This should be an offer that is crystal clear and compelling, outlining the many reasons why the other company should work with you as a partner.

It is essential to be succinct and get right to the point when you are formulating your partnership proposal. You need to explain the benefits of the partnership in a way that is simple enough for the other company to comprehend while also drawing their attention to what you have to say. This means avoiding language that is overly technical or complicated and concentrating instead on the advantages offered by the partnership.

In your presentation, it is essential to be as specific as possible. Give specific examples of how the partnership can benefit both businesses, as well as what you bring to the table, and what you bring to the table. This may take the form of case studies of fruitful partnerships in which you have participated or examples of how your expertise has assisted other businesses in achieving their goals.

When developing your business proposal for a partnership, it is critical to ensure that you are well-prepared to address any questions or concerns that may arise. Anticipate any objections that the other company might have and be prepared with responses that are crystal clear and to the point. This will show that you have thought the partnership through and that you are prepared to address any issues that may come up in the future.

When developing your partnership proposal, tone and delivery are two additional important factors to take into consideration. You should communicate your excitement about working together with the partnership by showing that you are enthusiastic and passionate about the partnership. By doing so, you will be able to establish a good rapport with the other company and make a favorable first impression.

In conclusion, it is essential to follow up after delivering your pitch. Send a message or email of gratitude to the other company, and offer any additional information they might require. This will demonstrate to us both your commitment to the partnership as well as your professionalism.

To summarize, developing a compelling partnership pitch is absolutely necessary if one wishes to make a favorable first impression with prospective partners. Determine your goals and what you have to offer the other company, be succinct and specific, be ready to address concerns, and deliver your presentation with enthusiasm and a sense of passion. After you have given your presentation, demonstrate both your professionalism and your dedication to the partnership by following up.

Chapter 6: Nurturing Your Partnerships: Cultivating Strong Relationships

It is essential to nurture your partnerships if you want to build healthy, long-lasting relationships with your partners. Trust, continuous communication, and productive collaboration are necessary ingredients for a fruitful partnership. In this chapter, we will cover how to nurture your partnerships and provide practical advice for cultivating strong relationships with your partners. In addition, we will discuss how to nurture your partnerships.

The establishment of open lines of communication should serve as the initial step in the process of cultivating your partnerships. This includes having regular check-ins, providing updates on the progress being made towards your partnership goals, and having an ongoing conversation about how you can support each other in the most effective manner. It is essential to devise a communication strategy that is conducive to the operation of both businesses, in addition to being responsive and punctual in your communication.

Creating opportunities for collaboration is a vitally important component of fostering your partnerships and should not be overlooked. This means combining forces in terms of resources, expertise, and networks in order to accomplish common goals. Maintain consistent communication and cooperation with your business partners in order to generate new opportunities for everyone's benefit.

Additionally, it is essential to take the initiative to provide support for your partners. This requires you to look for ways in which you can assist them in accomplishing their objectives and provide value that goes above and beyond the terms of the partnership agreement you two have established. Your proactive support will help to build trust and strengthen the relationship between you and the other person.

It is essential to maintain an open and honest communication style when cultivating your partnerships. This entails being forthright about any difficulties or problems that may crop up and cooperating with one another to find answers or solutions. Being open and honest about your own goals and the ways in which the partnership will help you achieve them should also be a priority.

Recognizing and celebrating successes is another essential component of maintaining healthy relationships with your partners. Take the time to celebrate together whenever your partnership reaches a new benchmark or makes significant headway toward achieving its objectives. This will help to create a positive relationship and contribute to the development of camaraderie.

In addition to this, it is essential to conduct regular assessments of the efficiency of your collaboration and to adapt your approach accordingly. This entails keeping track of how far along you are in the process of achieving the goals you set for your partnership, analyzing the communication and collaboration that takes place between your companies, and making adjustments that will make your partnership more efficient.

Last but not least, it is essential to acknowledge the value of your partnership and to promote it to additional parties. Sharing your successes and promoting the other company to your existing clientele and professional contacts is an essential part of this strategy. This can assist in the development of your reputation and the expansion of your influence within your sector of the market.

In a nutshell, cultivating healthy relationships with your partners is crucial to the process of developing solid, long-term bonds with those you work with. To accomplish this goal requires open and honest communication, consistent teamwork, and faith. Your support should be proactive, your communication should be open and transparent, and you should recognize and celebrate your successes together. Maintain a regular evaluation schedule to assess the efficacy of your partnership and make necessary adjustments. You can build your reputation and increase your influence within your industry by spreading the word about your partnership with other people.

Chapter 7: Overcoming Partnership Challenges: Resolving Conflict and Disagreements

There is no such thing as a flawless partnership; arguments and disagreements are unavoidable. Nevertheless, the way in which you respond to these challenges will either ensure the success or ensure the failure of your partnership. In this chapter, we will discuss how to overcome challenges that arise in partnerships and provide advice that can be put into practice to resolve conflict and differences of opinion.

Recognizing the problem is the first step toward finding solutions to the difficulties that arise in partnerships. This requires being open and honest about any differences of opinion or disagreements that may arise, as well as addressing them in a timely manner while maintaining a respectful demeanor. When trying to resolve disagreements, it is essential to devise a communication strategy, as well as to be responsive and timely in your communication.

When addressing a conflict or a difference of opinion, it is essential to keep one's attention on the matter at hand and to refrain from making personal attacks. This requires keeping a level head and avoiding language that is overly emotional. In addition to this, it is essential to give careful attention to the viewpoint of the other party and to make an effort to comprehend their position.

It is essential to keep an open mind and investigate a number of potential resolutions before attempting to settle a dispute or disagreement if at all possible. This entails generating a list of potential solutions and locating a solution that is satisfactory to both parties involved. It is essential that both parties be willing to compromise and actively seek ways to accommodate the requirements of the other.

When difficulties cannot be resolved internally, it may be beneficial to seek assistance from a third party or participate in a mediation process. This may involve bringing in a neutral third party to act as a mediator or seeking advice from a respected colleague or an expert in the relevant industry. It is vitally important to be willing to seek assistance from outside sources whenever it is required in order to guarantee that the conflict or disagreement will be resolved in a manner that is fair and equitable.

It is also essential to gain insight from arguments and disagreements and to take measures to forestall the recurrence of problems with a comparable nature in the future. This entails conducting an analysis of the efficacy of your communication and collaboration, as well as making necessary adjustments, in order to boost the efficiency of your partnership.

In conclusion, it is essential to acknowledge the value of your partnership and to maintain a focus on the objectives that you have jointly established. It is easy to lose perspective of the bigger picture when there are disagreements or conflicts taking place. Nevertheless, it is essential to keep your attention on the goals you have set together and to collaborate in order to accomplish them.

To summarize, overcoming the challenges presented by a partnership requires acknowledging the existence of conflicts and disagreements, maintaining a focus on the matter at hand, actively listening to the perspective of the other party, investigating multiple solutions, being willing to compromise, seeking mediation or assistance from a third party when necessary, learning from conflicts and disagreements, and maintaining a focus on your shared goals. If you follow these steps, you will be able to resolve disagreements and conflicts in a manner that is respectful and equitable, and you will be able to keep on building a productive partnership.

Chapter 8: Measuring Partnership Success: How to Determine if It's Working

It is essential to measure the success of partnerships in order to evaluate the efficiency of partnerships and make necessary adjustments. It is critical to establish transparent metrics for measuring success and to conduct regular evaluations of your partnership's progress toward achieving its goals. In this chapter, we will talk about how to measure the success of a partnership and provide some helpful advice for determining whether or not your partnership is functioning properly.

Establishing clear metrics for measuring progress towards your partnership goals should be the first step in the process of measuring the success of your partnership. This could include things like sales, website traffic, customer engagement, or any number of other metrics that are pertinent to the objectives of your partnership. At the beginning of your partnership, it is essential to determine a baseline for these metrics and to monitor your progress over the course of the relationship.

Once you have determined the metrics that will be used to evaluate success, it is imperative that you evaluate your partnership's progress toward its goals on a regular basis. This entails scheduling periodic checkpoints at which you will evaluate your progress and make necessary modifications. In addition to this, it is essential to communicate openly about the steps you are taking to achieve your goals and to address any problems that may crop up along the way.

It is essential to take into account both quantitative and qualitative metrics when conducting a success assessment of a partnership. You can get a clear picture of your progress toward your goals by using quantitative metrics, such as the number of sales or visitors to your website. However, the effectiveness of your partnership can also be evaluated using qualitative metrics, such as the level of satisfaction experienced by customers or the reputation enjoyed by a brand.

Assessing how well you communicate with one another and work together is another essential aspect to take into account when determining the level of success achieved by your partnership. This necessitates taking into consideration aspects such as the responsiveness, dependability, and quality of communication that exists between your companies. It is essential to conduct regular assessments of these aspects and to adapt your approach, as appropriate, in order to maximize the efficiency of your partnership.

It is essential that you take into account the effect that your partnership will have on the overarching goals of your company. Have you been able to accomplish your business goals with the assistance of the partnership, such as penetrating a new market or raising consumers' awareness of your brand? It is essential to perform regular assessments of the impact that your partnership has on the achievement of your overall business goals in order to confirm that it is, in fact, adding value to your company.

In conclusion, it is essential to take into account the level of contentment experienced by both parties involved in the partnership. Are both companies pleased with the partnership and the way it has helped them move closer to achieving their respective goals? Checking in with your business partner on a regular basis and asking for their input are two ways to help ensure that both companies are happy with the partnership they have formed.

To summarize, measuring the success of a partnership requires establishing clear metrics for measuring progress towards your partnership goals, regularly evaluating progress, taking into consideration both quantitative and qualitative metrics, evaluating the effectiveness of your communication and collaboration, considering the impact on your overall business objectives, and taking into consideration the satisfaction of both parties involved in the partnership. You will be able to make any necessary adjustments to your partnership if you regularly assess its performance and ensure that it is contributing positively to your company by conducting this evaluation.

Chapter 9: Growing Your Business with Strategic Partnerships: Success Stories and Lessons Learned

By capitalizing on the combined capabilities of a number of different companies, the growth of individual businesses may be significantly accelerated through the formation of strategic partnerships. In this chapter, we will discuss the success stories of businesses that have grown through strategic partnerships, as well as the lessons that those businesses have learned.

The partnership that has been formed between Apple and Nike is an excellent illustration of a productive strategic alliance. In 2006, Nike introduced a new line of running shoes to the market that were compatible with the iPod sold by Apple. Integrated into the runner's shoes was a sensor that monitored their performance and relayed that information to their iPod so they could receive feedback in real time. This partnership not only resulted in increased value for Nike's running shoes but also contributed to an increase in the number of iPods that were purchased.

Starbucks and Spotify have formed a successful strategic partnership, which is another example of a successful strategic partnership. A partnership between Starbucks and Spotify was announced in 2015, and as a result, customers of Starbucks were given the ability to access Spotify playlists in-store as well as via the Starbucks mobile app. Customers of Starbucks received additional value as a result of this partnership, and engagement with Spotify increased as a direct result of this partnership's efforts.

The importance of identifying complementary strengths and finding ways to leverage those strengths to achieve shared objectives is one of the lessons that can be learned from the development of successful strategic partnerships. Additionally, it is essential to establish open lines of communication, as well as a willingness to collaborate and make concessions. In conclusion, it is essential to conduct regular assessments of the efficiency of the partnership and to make necessary modifications based on the results of these assessments.

However, not all strategic alliances end up being fruitful in the end. One example of a partnership that did not work out is the one that was formed between Google and Nest. Google completed its acquisition of the smart home technology company Nest in 2014 with the intention of integrating Nest's products with those of Google's already-existing offerings. The integration, on the other hand, was executed poorly and failed to offer anything of value to customers; as a result, sales were disappointing and customers were dissatisfied.

The importance of clearly defining objectives and expectations before entering into a partnership is one of the most important things that can be learned from strategic partnerships that have been attempted but ultimately failed. In addition, it is essential to create a structure for decision-making and to perform regular evaluations of the efficacy of the partnership in order to confirm that it is, in fact, beneficial to all of the parties involved.

To summarize, strategic partnerships have the potential to drive significant business growth by leveraging the strengths of multiple businesses. This can be accomplished by combining the strengths of the partnering companies. It is possible to gain useful insights into how to create successful partnerships by reading about past partnerships' achievements and the lessons that were learned, whether those partnerships were successful or not. Finding complementary strengths, establishing clear communication, being open to collaboration and compromise, and routinely evaluating the partnership's effectiveness are essential components of a successful outcome. Businesses are able to develop effective strategic partnerships that drive business growth when they apply the lessons learned from both their successes and their failures.

Chapter 10: The Dos and Don'ts of Partnership Recruiting: Best Practices for Building Strong Alliances

The recruitment of partners is an essential step in the construction of robust partnerships, which in turn drive business expansion. However, in order to successfully recruit the right partners, a strategic approach and strict adherence to best practices are required. In this chapter, we will cover the dos and don'ts of partnership recruiting and provide advice that can be put into practice in order to create strong alliances.

Dos:

Clearly define your partnership goals and objectives before beginning the process of recruiting new partners. It is important to clearly define your partnership goals and objectives before beginning the recruitment process. This will assist you in determining the kinds of partners that are a good fit for your company in the best possible way.

Determine which strengths are complementary to those of your business and look for partners whose businesses have strengths that are complementary to your own. This will be helpful in the formation of a partnership that is of value and benefits to both parties.

Perform due diligence: Prior to entering into a partnership, it is important to perform due diligence on potential partners in order to ensure that they align with your values and goals. This may include researching the reputation of the individual in question, conducting interviews, and checking references.

Establish clear communication Once you have identified potential partners, the next step is to establish clear communication channels in order to discuss the goals and expectations you have for your partnership. Before entering into a partnership, this will help to ensure that both parties are on the same page and have the same expectations.

Maintain a willingness to collaborate with others and make concessions; successful partnerships require both of these qualities. Maintain an open mind to the thoughts and recommendations of your collaborators, and demonstrate a willingness to compromise in order to accomplish your goals together.

Don'ts:

Be impatient with the process of recruiting: Being impatient with the process of recruiting can lead to selecting the wrong partners or entering into partnerships that do not align with your objectives. Spend some time doing your research and giving potential partners careful consideration before making any decisions.

Neglect to consider compatibility: When searching for business partners, it is essential to take into account compatibility in addition to complementary strengths. If you want your partnership to be successful, you need to make sure that your values, communication preferences, and cultural backgrounds are compatible.

Be excessively focused on the gains in the short term: While it is necessary to identify partners who can provide immediate benefits, it is also essential to take into consideration long-term goals. Search for potential business partners who can offer your company long-term value and benefits that will continue to accrue.

Inability to set clear expectations: Partnerships have the potential to quickly become ineffective or even harmful if clear expectations and communication are not established. It is important to ensure that both parties are working toward the same goals from the beginning of the partnership, so it is important to establish clear expectations and goals.

Overcommit or underdeliver: It is essential to avoid either of these two pitfalls by being realistic about what you can provide to your partners and avoiding either overcommitting or underdelivering. Be truthful about what you are able to contribute, and strive to achieve goals that are attainable.

In conclusion, partnership recruiting necessitates an approach that is strategic as well as a strict adherence to best practices. Dos consist of things like clearly defining the goals of the partnership, finding complementary strengths, conducting due diligence, establishing clear communication, and being open to collaboration and compromise. Important things that shouldn't be done include things like rushing through the hiring process, failing to consider compatibility, being overly focused on short-term gains, failing to establish clear expectations, and overcommitting or underdelivering. Businesses have the ability to build strong alliances that drive growth if they adhere to these best practices and follow them.

Chapter 11: Creating Win-Win Partnerships: How to Ensure Mutually Beneficial Agreements

A partnership is said to be win-win when it results in mutually beneficial outcomes for both parties involved. It is important to establish clear goals and to identify ways in which both parties can provide value to each other in order to create a partnership that benefits everyone involved. This will help ensure that everyone involved comes out ahead. In this chapter, we will examine how to ensure that agreements are beneficial to both parties and provide advice that can be put into practice when developing win-win partnerships.

Clearly defining your goals and locating areas in which you can both benefit is the first step in developing a partnership that is beneficial for both parties. This requires you to think about what you want to get out of the partnership as well as how your business can benefit from the contributions your partner can make. In order to ensure that a partnership will be successful and can continue into the future, it is essential to define both short-term and long-term goals.

When you have determined the areas in which you and your partner will both benefit, the next step is to establish clear expectations for the partnership. This requires the establishment of distinct roles and responsibilities, as well as timetables, for the accomplishment of agreed-upon goals. In order to guarantee that both parties are working toward the same goals, it is essential to devise a structure for making decisions and resolving conflicts.

Maintaining an open and honest line of communication is another essential component to establishing a successful partnership that benefits both parties. This requires you to communicate with your partner on a regular basis, share your goals and expectations with them, and be responsive to their questions and concerns. It is essential to schedule regular check-ins to evaluate your progress toward your goals and to determine whether or not any alterations are required.

It is essential to be flexible and willing to find ways to accommodate one another's requirements during the process of negotiating the terms of a partnership agreement. This entails maintaining an attitude that is receptive to novel approaches and searching for additional avenues through which value can be provided in addition to that which was stipulated in the original partnership agreement. In order to accomplish goals that are important to both parties, it is essential to demonstrate a willingness to compromise.

In conclusion, it is essential to conduct regular assessments of the efficiency of the partnership and to make necessary modifications based on the results of these assessments. This entails keeping track of how far along you are in the process of achieving your goals, assessing how well you communicate with one another and work together, and adapting the partnership so that it functions more efficiently.

To summarize, developing a win-win partnership requires clearly defining your goals, locating areas in which you can both benefit, establishing clear expectations and roles, communicating in an open and transparent manner, demonstrating a willingness to compromise, and performing regular evaluations of the partnership's efficacy. By adhering to these best practices, companies can increase their chances of developing successful and long-lasting partnerships that are of value and benefit to both parties.

Chapter 12: The Role of Trust in Successful Partnerships: Building Rapport and Respect

---

Building and maintaining mutual trust is one of the most important factors in business partnerships. Without trust, communication and collaboration can be challenging, and partnerships can rapidly deteriorate into ones that are ineffective at best or even harmful at worst. In this chapter, we will talk about the importance of trust in productive partnerships and give some useful tips on how to develop rapport and respect for one another.

Establishing rapport and respect with one another is the first step in constructing trust within a partnership. This entails making the effort to learn about one's partner and to construct one's relationship on the foundation of respect and comprehension on both sides. This can include sharing personal stories, talking about interests that are shared, and looking for other ways to connect on a more personal level.

Being open and honest in your communication is another essential step in the process of constructing trust within a collaborative relationship. This requires you to communicate in a manner that is truthful and open, without withholding information or engaging in any kind of deception. In order to create a feeling of dependability and reliability, it is essential to communicate in a way that is both timely and responsive.

Building trust in a partnership also requires consistent behavior from both parties. This entails being reliable in your actions and following through in a consistent manner on the commitments you make. In addition to this, it is essential to maintain coherence in your communication and to schedule regular check-ins to go over the status of the project and make necessary adjustments.

In order to have a successful partnership, it is critical to lay out clear roles and responsibilities, in addition to developing mutual respect and rapport with one another. This requires you to be crystal clear about the goals and expectations you have for the relationship, as well as ensuring that both parties have a solid grasp of the roles and responsibilities that have been assigned to them. In order to guarantee that both parties are working toward the same goals, it is essential to devise a structure for making decisions and resolving conflicts.

Being willing to make concessions and work together to find solutions that satisfy the requirements of both parties is another essential component of establishing trust in a business partnership. This entails maintaining an attitude that is receptive to novel approaches and searching for additional avenues through which value can be provided in addition to that which was stipulated in the original partnership agreement. In order to accomplish goals that are important to both parties, it is essential to demonstrate a willingness to compromise.

In conclusion, it is essential to conduct regular assessments of the efficiency of the partnership and to make necessary modifications based on the results of these assessments. This entails keeping an eye on how well you are doing in terms of reaching your goals, assessing how well you communicate with one another and work together, and making adjustments so as to boost the efficiency of the partnership.

In a nutshell, trust is an indispensable quality for productive business relationships. Establishing clear expectations and roles, being willing to compromise, and routinely evaluating the partnership's effectiveness are all important factors in building trust. Other important factors include developing rapport and respect for one another, being transparent in your communication, remaining consistent in your actions and communication, and establishing clear expectations and roles. Businesses have a better chance of forming successful partnerships if they adhere to these best practices and do so in a way that benefits both parties.

Chapter 13: Finding the Right Partners: Identifying the Right Fit for Your Business

It is absolutely necessary for the success of any strategic partnership to locate the appropriate partners. However, it may not always be easy to determine which candidate is best suited for your company. In this chapter, we will discuss how to identify the appropriate business partners for your company, and we will provide advice on how to find the partners who are the best fit.

The first thing you need to do in order to find the right partners is to define your partnership goals and objectives in as much detail as possible. This requires you to think about what you want to get out of the partnership as well as how your business can benefit from the contributions your partner can make. In order to ensure that a partnership will be successful and can continue into the future, it is essential to define both short-term and long-term goals.

After you have established the objectives you wish to achieve through your partnerships, the next step is to think about the kinds of partners who would be most suitable for your company. This means finding partners who have strengths that are complementary to those of your company and who can assist you in achieving the goals you have set for yourself. In order to ensure that a partnership will be successful, it is essential to take into account a variety of factors, including cultural compatibility, communication styles, and values that are congruent.

Performing due diligence research on prospective business partners is an additional essential step in the process of finding the best partners. This entails conducting research into their reputation, conducting interviews, and checking references in order to guarantee that they are congruent with your values and goals. To ensure that they are a suitable partner for your company, it is essential to examine the financial security of the company as well as its position in the market.

Building relationships with potential business allies is another crucial step in the process. This entails participating in events hosted by your industry, joining organizations that are pertinent to your field, and networking with other professionals working in your field. You will be able to discover prospective partners and cultivate relationships that have the potential to result in fruitful collaborations if you build a robust network.

In addition to building relationships with other people, it is essential to make initial contact with prospective business partners. This entails locating prospective partners and making contact with them to inquire about available opportunities for collaboration. It is essential to have a crystal-clear understanding of your goals and expectations, as well as to construct a structure for making decisions and resolving conflicts.

Last but not least, it is essential to conduct regular assessments of the efficiency of your collaborations and to adapt your approach accordingly. This entails keeping track of how far along you are in the process of achieving your goals, assessing how well you communicate with one another and work together, and adapting the partnership so that it functions more efficiently.

In conclusion, in order to locate the most suitable partners, one must take a strategic approach and strictly adhere to standard operating procedures. Finding the right partner for your company requires you to clearly define your partnership goals, identify complementary strengths, perform due diligence, network, be proactive in reaching out to potential partners, and evaluate the partnership's effectiveness on a regular basis. All of these are important factors. Businesses are able to build fruitful partnerships that contribute to their expansion if they adhere to the best practices outlined here.

Chapter 14: Collaborating for Growth: Partnering with Competitors and Complementary Businesses

It is possible for businesses to achieve significant growth by working together with their rivals and businesses that complement one another. Businesses have the potential to increase their market share, reduce costs, and share resources if they form partnerships with their rivals. Businesses are able to broaden the range of products they offer and enter new markets if they form partnerships with companies that offer complementary goods and services. In this chapter, we will discuss the benefits of collaborating with competitors and complementary businesses, as well as the challenges that come along with doing so, and we will provide advice on how to have successful collaborations.

There are many advantages that can be gained by businesses by forming partnerships with their rivals. Businesses have the potential to cut costs and improve efficiencies by pooling their resources. Businesses are able to develop new goods and services that are in a better position to compete successfully in the market if they combine their respective areas of expertise and capabilities. The establishment of industry standards and regulations, which are of mutual benefit to all businesses operating within an industry, can also be facilitated by collaboration.

However, there are also difficulties involved when working together with other competitors. To collaborate effectively, there must be mutual trust and openness on the part of businesses, as well as a willingness to share information and resources. Businesses need to make sure that they are not engaging in anti-competitive behavior when they collaborate with one another, which can be difficult from a legal and regulatory point of view.

Businesses can reap a number of benefits from partnering with other companies that offer complementary products or services. Businesses are able to broaden their product offerings and enter new markets if they form partnerships with other companies whose strengths are complementary to their own. Through the sharing of resources and expertise, collaboration can also help to cut costs while simultaneously increasing efficiency.

However, there are also difficulties involved when collaborating with businesses that have complementary offerings. For two people to successfully collaborate, they need to have a solid understanding of each other's capabilities, as well as a willingness to share their resources and their expertise. When working together, it's important for businesses to make sure they have a strong cultural fit and a shared vision for the partnership. If they don't, collaboration can be difficult from a cultural standpoint as well.

It is important to establish clear goals and expectations before beginning any kind of collaboration with businesses that are either competitors or complementary to your own. This requires determining the objectives of the partnership, determining the roles and responsibilities of each participant, and determining the potential difficulties and dangers involved. In order to guarantee that both parties are working toward the same goals, it is essential to devise a structure for making decisions and resolving conflicts.

Communication is an additional crucial component that contributes to the success of teamwork. This entails setting up channels of communication that are unambiguous, as well as being responsive and punctual in your communications. In order to ensure that both parties are working toward the same goals, it is important to conduct regular check-ins to discuss the progress that has been made and to make adjustments as necessary.

In conclusion, it is essential to conduct regular assessments of the efficiency of the partnership and to make necessary modifications based on the results of these assessments. This entails keeping track of how far along you are in the process of achieving your goals, assessing how well you communicate with one another and work together, and adapting the partnership so that it functions more efficiently.

In a nutshell, a powerful growth strategy for businesses can be found in the practice of collaborating with complementary businesses and even competitors. Businesses have the potential to increase their market share, reduce costs, and share resources if they form partnerships with their rivals. Businesses are able to broaden the range of products they offer and enter new markets if they form partnerships with companies that offer complementary goods and services. A successful collaboration requires a number of important factors to come together, including the establishment of clear objectives and expectations, communication, and the routine evaluation of the partnership's effectiveness.

Chapter 15: The Legal Side of Partnerships: Understanding Contracts and Agreements

Legal contracts are necessary for partnerships because they ensure that both parties are on the same page regarding their respective roles, responsibilities, and expectations. In this chapter, we will discuss the significance of legally binding contracts and agreements in partnerships, as well as offer some useful recommendations for gaining an understanding of these documents and negotiating their terms.

To begin the process of drafting a legal agreement for a partnership, the first thing that must be done is to precisely define the goals and requirements of the partnership. This requires determining what each party expects to gain from the partnership as well as what roles each party intends to play in the partnership. It is important to ensure that both parties have a common understanding of the partnership's objectives and to state your goals in a way that is both clear and specific.

It is important to draft a legal agreement that outlines the terms of the partnership once the goals and expectations have been identified. This can be done once the objectives and expectations have been identified. This agreement ought to include specifics regarding the roles and responsibilities of each party, timelines for achieving common goals, and a structure for making decisions and resolving conflicts. The agreement ought to also include provisions for terminating the relationship and resolving any disputes that may arise.

When negotiating a legal agreement, it is essential to have a firm grasp on your goals and expectations, as well as the flexibility to make concessions in order to arrive at a settlement that is beneficial to both parties. In order to guarantee the safety of your company, it is essential to take into account a variety of elements, including liability and indemnification, intellectual property, and confidentiality.

In addition to this, it is essential to make certain that the legal agreement can be upheld in court and complies with all of the applicable laws and regulations. This entails consulting with legal counsel in order to ascertain that the agreement is legally enforceable and complies with all applicable laws and regulations.

In order to ensure that the legal agreement continues to be useful and effective over time, it is essential to regularly review it and bring it up to date. This entails keeping an eye on how well you are doing in terms of reaching your goals, assessing how well you communicate with one another and work together, and making adjustments so as to boost the efficiency of the partnership.

In conclusion, legally binding contracts and agreements are absolutely necessary for the progress and prosperity of partnerships. In order to create an efficient legal agreement for a partnership, it is necessary to clearly define the goals and expectations of the partnership, to draft a legal agreement that outlines the terms of the partnership, to negotiate a mutually beneficial agreement, to ensure compliance with applicable laws and regulations, and to routinely review and update the agreement. If businesses adhere to these best practices, they will be able to form partnerships that are not only successful but also long-lasting, providing value and benefits to both parties.

Chapter 16: Leveraging Partnerships for Marketing Success: Collaborative Campaigns and Strategies

For a company's marketing efforts to be successful, strategic partnerships can be an extremely useful tool. Businesses have the ability to expand their customer bases, raise their customers' awareness of their brands, and develop cutting-edge marketing strategies when they work together with other organizations. In this chapter, we will discuss the benefits of leveraging partnerships for marketing success as well as the challenges that come along with it. Additionally, we will provide some practical advice for developing successful collaborative campaigns and strategies.

Finding partners who have complementary strengths and who are able to assist you in achieving your marketing goals is the first step in the process of leveraging partnerships for marketing success. This means finding partners who have the same target audience as you do, values that are comparable to your own, and a strong cultural fit. It is essential to locate business partners who can assist you in expanding your customer base and who can add value to the operations of your company.

Once you have identified potential partners, the next step is to develop a marketing strategy that is crystal clear and outlines the goals of the partnership as well as the expectations that come along with it. This requires determining what the goals of the campaign are, determining who will be responsible for what aspects of the campaign, and developing a timeline for accomplishing the goals that everyone has agreed upon. In order to guarantee that both parties are working toward the same goals, it is essential to devise a structure for making decisions and resolving conflicts.

Communication is another crucial component that contributes to the success of marketing partnerships. This entails setting up channels of communication that are unambiguous, as well as being responsive and punctual in your communications. In order to ensure that both parties are working toward the same goals, it is important to conduct regular check-ins to discuss the progress that has been made and to make adjustments as necessary.

It is essential to work together with other people to create marketing materials and campaigns, in addition to communicating effectively. This entails drawing upon one another's areas of expertise and strengths in order to create marketing campaigns that are original and effective. It is also essential to devise a consistent branding strategy for the partnership that takes into account the values and capabilities of both partners.

It is also essential to evaluate the efficiency of the collaborative marketing strategies and campaigns that have been implemented. In order to determine whether or not the campaign was successful, it is necessary to monitor certain key performance indicators, such as engagement, conversions, and revenue. In addition to this, it is essential to conduct regular assessments of the performance of the partnership and to make appropriate adjustments.

However, there are also obstacles to overcome when attempting to leverage partnerships in order to achieve marketing success. For collaborative marketing campaigns to be successful, both parties involved need to have a solid understanding of each other's capabilities, as well as a willingness to share resources, knowledge, and expertise. When working together, it's important for businesses to make sure they have a strong cultural fit and a shared vision for the partnership. If they don't, collaboration can be difficult from a cultural standpoint as well.

In conclusion, it is necessary to take a strategic approach and adhere to best practices in order to achieve success in marketing by leveraging partnerships. Effective collaborative marketing campaigns and strategies require a number of important factors to come together in order to be successful. These factors include clearly defining the goals and expectations of the partnership, communicating and working together, measuring the effectiveness of the partnership, and evaluating its effectiveness on a regular basis. Businesses are able to establish fruitful and long-lasting partnerships that not only contribute to the expansion of their operations but also raise consumers' awareness of their brands if these best practices are followed.

Chapter 17: The Importance of Communication in Partnerships: Ensuring Clear and Consistent Dialogue

It is essential to the success of partnerships to maintain communication that is both clear and consistent. In this chapter, we will go over the significance of communication in business partnerships and offer some useful suggestions for ensuring that dialogue is both clear and consistent.

Establishing channels of communication that are unambiguous and unambiguous is the first step in ensuring clear and consistent communication. This entails determining which communication tools and platforms are the most useful for your partnership. These could include email, the phone, video conferencing, or software designed for collaboration. It is essential to set up a regular communication schedule and to make certain that both parties are aware of the communication channels that are preferred by the other.

Establishing expectations for response times is another essential part of clear and consistent communication that should not be overlooked. This entails establishing crystal-clear expectations for how quickly partners should respond to communication and how to handle pressing issues. It is essential to make certain that both parties are aware of these expectations and that they are conveyed in a straightforward manner.

It is essential to guarantee that communication is both clear and efficient, in addition to determining the channels of communication and response times that will be used. This requires you to communicate in a way that is crystal clear and to the point, stay away from jargon and other forms of technical language, and provide context when it is required. It is essential to show your partner that you are actively listening to them and that you are making an effort to comprehend the world from their point of view.

In order to ensure that both parties are working toward the same goals, it is important to conduct regular check-ins to discuss the progress that has been made and to make adjustments as necessary. It is essential to set up regular touchpoints, such as meetings once a week or once a month, in order to monitor progress and make necessary adjustments as they come up.

Establishing a framework for decision-making and conflict resolution is another essential component of effective communication. This requires determining the procedure for making decisions, ensuring that both parties are given an opportunity to participate in the procedure, and devising a plan for mediating disagreements between the parties. It is essential to ensure that both parties are aware of the decision-making process as well as the framework for conflict resolution, and that this information is communicated in an understandable manner.

In conclusion, it is essential to conduct regular assessments of the efficiency of communication within the partnership and to make necessary modifications based on the results of these assessments. This entails keeping track of how well goals are being met, determining how well communication and collaboration are working, and adapting strategies as necessary in order to enhance the efficiency of the partnership.

In conclusion, it is essential for the success of partnerships to have communication that is both clear and consistent. A clear and consistent dialogue is achieved through the establishment of clear communication channels, expectations for response times, clear and effective communication, regular check-ins, a framework for decision-making and conflict resolution, and the routine evaluation of the effectiveness of communication. All of these factors are important in ensuring a clear and consistent dialogue. By adhering to these best practices, companies can increase their chances of developing successful and long-lasting partnerships that are of value and benefit to both parties.

Chapter 18: The Future of Partnership Recruiting: Trends and Predictions for the Evolving Business Landscape

However, the landscape is always shifting, making partnership recruiting an effective growth strategy for businesses despite the fact that the landscape is always changing. In this chapter, we will discuss trends and predictions for the future of partnership recruiting in light of the shifting landscape of the business world.

Utilizing various forms of technology in order to more easily form partnerships is currently emerging as one of the most prominent trends in partnership recruitment. The use of digital platforms and tools can assist businesses in locating potential partners, streamlining communication and collaboration, and determining the degree to which partnerships are successful. As a result of the ongoing development of technology, businesses can anticipate the appearance of an increasing number of tools and platforms created expressly for the purpose of partnership recruitment.

The use of data to inform partnership decisions is one more trend that can be seen in partnership recruiting. Businesses are able to identify potential partners that have complementary strengths and that can contribute to the achievement of shared objectives by analyzing data such as the behavior of customers, trends in the market, and regulations governing the industry. Data analysis can also assist businesses in determining the efficacy of their partnerships and in making data-driven decisions regarding their future collaborations with other businesses.

Partnerships are becoming more international in scope as businesses continue to expand their operations across the globe. Because of this, companies need to be aware of the cultural norms and laws that exist in a variety of countries, and they also need to be able to communicate effectively despite the linguistic and cultural barriers that exist. Those companies and organizations that are capable of overcoming these obstacles will have an advantage over their competitors in the international market.

The growth of social entrepreneurship is also driving changes in the recruitment practices of partnership organizations. Partnerships with other companies that share the same values as social entrepreneurs can help to magnify the positive impact that these entrepreneurs have on their communities and the natural environment through the work they do in their businesses. Companies that place a high priority on their social and environmental responsibilities can anticipate an increase in the number of partnership opportunities available in this field.

Lastly, the ongoing COVID-19 pandemic is causing changes in the recruitment practices of partnership organizations. The importance of virtual collaboration tools and platforms has been growing in recent years as the number of businesses that operate remotely has increased. In the world that has recovered from the pandemic, businesses that are able to effectively leverage virtual collaboration tools and platforms will have a competitive advantage when it comes to recruiting partners.

To summarize, partnership recruiting is a powerful growth strategy for businesses, but the landscape is constantly evolving, making it difficult to make accurate predictions. Changes in partnership recruiting are being driven by a number of factors, including the internationalization of partnerships, the rise of social entrepreneurship, the ongoing COVID-19 pandemic, and the use of technology to facilitate partnerships; the use of data to inform partnership decisions; and the use of data to inform partnership decisions. In the future, businesses that are able to successfully navigate these changes and capitalize on emerging trends will have a competitive advantage when it comes to partnership recruiting.

Chapter 19: Scaling Your Business with Partnerships: How to Build a Network for Sustainable Growth

The expansion of your company and the achievement of sustainable growth can both be significantly aided by forming strategic partnerships. In this chapter, we will go over the steps necessary to construct a network of partnerships that can propel your company's growth in a sustainable direction.

To begin developing a network of partnerships, the first thing you need to do is make your objectives and goals crystal clear. This means determining the areas in which you require assistance and the kinds of partners who can assist you in achieving the goals that you have set for yourself. It is essential to find business partners who have complementary strengths and who are able to add value to your company.

It is essential to formulate a distinct plan for the partnership once you have identified potential partners in the market. This requires the establishment of clear roles and responsibilities, as well as the formulation of a timetable for the accomplishment of goals that are held in common, before the partnership can be considered successful. In order to guarantee that both parties are working toward the same goals, it is essential to devise a structure for making decisions and resolving conflicts.

Communication is an additional essential component in the process of developing a network of partnership relationships. This entails setting up channels of communication that are unambiguous, as well as being responsive and punctual in your communications. In order to ensure that both parties are working toward the same goals, it is important to conduct regular check-ins to discuss the progress that has been made and to make adjustments as necessary.

In addition to maintaining open lines of communication, it is critical to work together in order to create successful products, services, and marketing campaigns. This entails drawing upon one another's areas of expertise and strengths in order to come up with creative and game-changing solutions for the customers. In addition to this, it is essential to devise a consistent branding strategy for the partnership that takes into account the values and capabilities of both partners.

The evaluation of the efficiency of the partnerships constitutes yet another essential component of the process of developing a network of collaborations. In order to determine how successful the partnership is, it is necessary to monitor certain key performance indicators, such as the level of engagement, the number of conversions, and the revenue. In addition to this, it is essential to conduct regular assessments of the performance of the partnership and to make appropriate adjustments.

It is essential to maintain relationships with your partners that are open and honest if you wish to construct a network of partnerships that will endure over time. This entails not only being open and forthright about your objectives and requirements, but also ensuring that the partnership is mutually beneficial to both parties involved. In addition to being willing to receive as well as give, it's critical to maintain an open mind toward potential new partnerships and opportunities.

In conclusion, it is essential to perform regular analyses of the efficacy of your network of partnership relationships and to adapt those analyses as circumstances demand. This entails keeping an eye on how well you are doing in terms of reaching your goals, determining how well you communicate with one another and work together, and making adjustments to your network of partnerships so that they are more efficient.

In a nutshell, the development of a partnership network is absolutely necessary for expanding the scope of one's business and achieving steady growth. Building a sustainable network of partnerships that drives business growth and success requires a number of important factors to be present. Some of these factors include clearly defining your objectives and goals, developing a clear partnership strategy, communicating and collaborating effectively, measuring effectiveness, maintaining open and transparent relationships, and regularly evaluating the effectiveness of your network of partnerships.

Chapter 20: Creating a Partnership Culture: Encouraging Collaboration and Innovation in Your Business

---

Establishing a culture of partnership within your company can be a catalyst for increased collaboration, innovation, and expansion. In this chapter, we will go over the best practices for establishing a culture of partnerships that fosters creativity and cooperation.

The first thing you need to do in order to establish a culture of collaboration is to emphasize the significance of partnerships to your team. This means that the benefits of partnerships, such as increased innovation, expanded reach, and increased revenue, must be communicated in a clear and concise manner. It is essential to ensure that your team has a solid understanding of the significance of partnerships and the ways in which these relationships can contribute to the success of the company.

Discovering the different ways in which your organization can work together effectively is an additional essential step in the process of developing a culture of partnership. This involves locating areas in which different teams can collaborate to develop innovative solutions for customers and identifying those areas. It is critical to instill a culture of openness and transparency within a team, one in which individuals are actively encouraged to contribute their thoughts and collaborate with one another to achieve the goals that have been set.

In addition to this, it is essential to promote an innovative mindset all throughout your organization. This means that members of the team should be encouraged to develop creative solutions to problems and to think creatively outside the box. It is essential to cultivate a setting in which mistakes are seen as educational opportunities and where a value is placed on experimentation and innovation.

It is essential to create open communication channels and processes for collaboration, in addition to cultivating an environment that encourages inventiveness and experimentation. This entails setting up checkpoints and meetings on a consistent basis in order to evaluate the state of things and make necessary adjustments. In addition to this, it is essential to define each member of the team's specific roles and responsibilities, as well as to ensure that they are aware of the team's preferred communication channels and response times.

Recognizing and celebrating successes is another essential step in the process of establishing a culture of collaboration. This entails recognizing the contributions made by members of the team and partners, as well as celebrating significant milestones and accomplishments. It is essential to establish a culture of positivity and celebration within the team in order to motivate individual members to contribute to the accomplishment of group aims and targets.

In conclusion, it is essential to make investments in the education and growth of the members of your team. Providing opportunities for members of the team to develop new skills and learn about emerging trends and best practices in partnership recruitment and collaboration is an essential part of achieving this goal. Creating a culture of never-ending improvement and innovation that propels the expansion and success of your company can be accomplished by investing in the members of your team.

Developing a culture of partnership is absolutely necessary if you want your company to experience increased levels of collaboration, innovation, and overall growth. Establishing clear communication channels and processes for collaboration, recognizing and celebrating successes, and investing in training and development are all important factors in creating a partnership culture that encourages collaboration and innovation within your organization. Communicating the importance of partnerships, identifying opportunities for collaboration, fostering a culture of innovation, establishing clear communication channels and processes for collaboration, and fostering a culture of innovation are all important factors. Businesses have the ability to create a culture of success and achievement that is the driving force behind sustained growth and success if they follow these best practices.

Also by B. Vincent

Affiliate Marketing
Affiliate Marketing
Affiliate Marketing

Standalone
Business Employee Discipline
Affiliate Recruiting
Business Layoffs & Firings
Business and Entrepreneur Guide
Business Remote Workforce
Career Transition
Project Management
Precision Targeting
Professional Development
Strategic Planning
Content Marketing
Imminent List Building
Getting Past GateKeepers
Banner Ads
Bookkeeping
Bridge Pages
Business Acquisition

Business Bogging
Business Communication Course
Marketing Automation
Better Meetings
Business Conflict Resolution
Business Culture Course
Conversion Optimization
Creative Solutions
Employee Recruitment
Startup Capital
Employee Incentives
Employee Mentoring
Followership
Servant Leadership
Human Resources
Team Building
Freelancing
Funnel Building
Geo Targeting
Goal Setting
Immanent List Building
Lead Generation
Leadership Course
Leadership Transition
Leadership vs Management
LinkedIn Ads
LinkedIn Marketing
Messenger Marketing
New Management
Newsfeed Ads
Search Ads
Online Learning
Sales Webinars

Side Hustles
Split Testing
Twitter Timeline Advertising
Earning Additional Income Through Side Hustles: Begin Earning Money Immediately
Making a Living Through Blogging: Earn Money Working From Home
Create Bonuses for Affiliate Marketing: Your Success Is Encompassed by Your Bonuses
Internet Marketing Success: The Most Effective Traffic-Driving Strategies
JV Recruiting: Joint Ventures Partnerships and Affiliates
Secrets to List Building
Step-by-Step Facebook Marketing: Discover How To Create A Strategy That Will Help You Grow Your Business
Banner Advertising: Traffic Can Be Boosted by Banner Ads
Affiliate Marketing
Improve Your Marketing Strategy with Internet Marketing
Outsourcing Helps You Save Time and Money
Choosing the Right Content and Marketing for Social Media
Make Products That Will Sell
Launching a Product for Affiliate Marketing
Pinterest as a Marketing Tool
Power Partnerships: Mastering the Art of Business Growth Through Partnership Recruiting

About the Publisher

Accepting manuscripts in the most categories. We love to help people get their words available to the world.

Revival Waves of Glory focus is to provide more options to be published. We do traditional paperbacks, hardcovers, audio books and ebooks all over the world. A traditional royalty-based publisher that offers self-publishing options, Revival Waves provides a very author friendly and transparent publishing process, with President Bill Vincent involved in the full process of your book. Send us your manuscript and we will contact you as soon as possible.

Contact: Bill Vincent at rwgpublishing@yahoo.com

www.ingramcontent.com/pod-product-compliance
Lightning Source LLC
LaVergne TN
LVHW041537060526
838200LV00037B/1026